Nita Mehta's

Drink & Indian Desserts

Nita Mehta

B.Sc. (Home Science), M.Sc. (Food and Nutrition) Gold Medalist

Drinks & Indian Desserts

Snab Publishers Pvt Ltd

Corporate Office
3A/3, Asaf Ali Road, New Delhi 110 002
Phone: +91 11 2325 2948, 2325 0091
Telefax: +91 11 2325 0091
E-mail: nitamehta@nitamehta.com
Website: www.nitamehta.com

© Copyright Snab Publishers Pvt Ltd 2009-2011
All rights reserved
ISBN 978-81-7869-305-7
Reprint 2011
Printed in India by Nutech Photolithographers
Cover desined by: flyingtrees

Distributed by: **NITA MEHTA BOOKS** — Distributors & Publishers
NITA MEHTA BOOKS
3A/3, Asaf Ali Road, New Delhi - 02
Distribution Centre :
D16/1, Okhla Industrial Area, Phase-I,
New Delhi - 110020
Tel.: 26813199, 26813200
E-mail: nitamehta.mehta@gmail.com

Editorial and Marketing office
E-159, Greater Kailash II, New Delhi 110 048

Food Styling and Photography by Snab
Typesetting by National Information Technology Academy
3A/3, Asaf Ali Road, New Delhi 110 002

Recipe Development & Testing:
Nita Mehta Foods - R & D Centre
3A/3, Asaf Ali Road, New Delhi - 110002
E-143, Amar Colony, Lajpat Nagar-IV, New Delhi - 110024

World rights reserved: The contents - all recipes, photographs and drawings are original and copyrighted. No portion of this book shall be reproduced, stored in a retrieval system or transmitted by any means, electronic, mechanical, photocopying, recording or otherwise, without the written permission of the publishers. While every precaution is taken in the preparation of this book, the publishers and the author assume no responsibility for errors or omissions. Neither is any liability assumed for damages resulting from the use of information contained herein.
TRADEMARKS ACKNOWLEDGED: Trademarks used, if any, are acknowledged as trademarks of their respective owners. These are used as reference only and no trademark infringement is intended upon. Ajinomoto (monosodium glutamade, MSG) is a trademark of Aji-no-moto company of Japan. Use it sparingly if you must as a flavour enhancer.

Price: Rs. 89/-

INTRODUCTION

Wondering how to chill out this season? Here are great recipes, too easy to be true, to delight you! All you need are a few common ingredients to churn out the most exotic drinks and desserts you have always desired.

Nowadays, a varied variety of ready-made fruit juices, fruit crushes, coconut milk, coconut water and fresh fruits are available in the market. The catch is - how can you combine them to get something really refreshing and fascinating!

The book includes a treasury of elegant sweet dishes including classic desserts as well as a good selection of the new ones. Entertain and surprise everyone with the sugary fragrance and eye appeal of these culinary triumphs.

Nita Mehta

Contents

WHAT'S IN A CUP?
INDIAN CUP   1 teacup = 200 ml liquid
AMERICAN CUP   1 cup = 240 ml liquid (8 oz.)
The recipes in this book were tested with the Indian teacup which holds 200 ml liquid.

Introduction 3

DRINKS   6

Rose Thandai 7	Kahwa 30
Jal Jeera 10	Magaz Rose Lassi 32
Strawberry Colada 12	Mango-Ginger Iced Tea 34
Orange Delight 14	Falooda 36
Nimboo Soda 16	Zafran Sherbet 38
Strawberry Mint Smoothie ... 18	Papaya Honey Smoothie 40
Sherbet Angoori 20	Lemonade Delight 42
Roasted Almond Milk Shake 22	Gajar ki Kanji 44
Cool Flavour 24	Pink Lady 46
Black Grape Cooler 26	Purple Rain 48
Summer Cool 28	Khus Punch 50
	Adraki Shikanjvi 52

INDIAN DESSERTS 54

Malpuas 55	Kulfi 78
Payasam 58	Makhane ki Rose Kheer 80
Anjeer Ice Cream 60	Paneer aur Petha ka Peda .. 82
Coconut Suji Ladoo 62	Moong Dal Halwa 85
Rasgulla Pudding 64	Kalakand 88
Fruit & Ice 66	Besan ki Burfi 90
Duet Ice Cream 68	Hyderabadi Cookies 92
Biscuit Pudding 70	Atta Pinnie 94
Anjeer aur Nariyal ki Barfi . 72	Kesari Sandesh 96
Rose Shahi Tukri 74	Mewa ke Ladoo 98
Jalebi with Rabri 76	Suji ka Halwa 100

HERBS AND SPICES 102
INTERNATIONAL CONVERSION GUIDE 103

DRINKS

Rose Thandai

A festive drink prepared from nuts and flavourful spices blended in milk.

Serves 8

7½ cups milk (1½ litres)
½ cup almonds
2 tbsp broken cashewnuts
1/3 cup seeds of watermelon (*magaz*)
8 tbsp poppy seeds (*khus khus*)
15-20 peppercorns (*saboot kali mirch*)
6-8 green cardamoms (*chhoti illaichi*)
¼ cup dried rose petals
10 tbsp rose syrup, or to taste

GARNISH

few strands of saffron (*kesar*) - soak in 1 tbsp warm water

1. Soak almonds separately in water for 3-4 hours.
2. Soak together — seeds of watermelon, poppy seeds, cashewnuts, peppercorns, cardamoms and rose petals for 3-4 hours. Strain.
3. Peel the almonds and add to the other ingredients. Put all the soaked ingredients in a mixer grinder and grind to a smooth paste by adding a little water or milk. The grinding of the ingredients should be done very well. Grind well 3-4 times to extract the juices as well as the flavour by adding some water or milk.
4. Add the ground ingredients to the cold milk.
5. Strain the milk through a muslin cloth and discard the residue.
6. Add rose syrup and mix well. Chill the thandai by adding ice.
7. Serve garnished with soaked kesar and rose petals.

Jal Jeera

This jal jeera is made with amchoor. You can also take 2-3 tbsp of tamarind pulp instead.

Serves 5-6

1½ tbsp dried mango (*amchoor*) powder
3 tbsp cumin seeds, roasted and ground (*bhuna jeera*)
2 tbsp black salt
6 tbsp lemon juice
6 tbsp powdered sugar
5 cups chilled water
4 tbsp fresh mint leaf paste, see note

GARNISH

2 tbsp *besan ki boondi*

Note: Grind a bunch of pudina leaves, 1 tsp chopped ginger and 2 tbsp coriander leaves with a little water to a paste and use 4 tbsp of this paste in the recipe.

1. Mix cumin seeds, mint paste, coriander paste, amchoor, black salt, lemon juice and sugar.
2. Add 5 cups of chilled water and stir till all the ingredients are well blended.
3. Pour into tall glasses, garnish with mint leaves and boondi, serve chilled.

Strawberry Colada

Serves 2

1 cup pineapple juice
½ cup coconut milk
1 tbsp strawberry crush
4 tsp finely grated fresh coconut
6-8 ice-cubes

GARNISH

a piece of fresh pineapple
some finely grated coconut
4 tsp strawberry crush

1. Blend the pineapple juice, coconut milk, strawberry crush and the ice-cubes in the blender till well blended.
2. Pour 2 tsp strawberry crush at the base of a glass.
3. Place crushed ice at the bottom of a cocktail glass and pour the blended mixture.
4. Sprinkle some grated coconut and arrange the pineapple slice on the rim of the glass.

Orange Delight

Serves 2

1½ cups mirinda
1 tbsp rose syrup
1 tbsp lemon juice
2 pinches of salt
½ tsp powdered sugar
½ cup vanilla ice-cream
few ice cubes

1. Blend all ingredients in a blender till smooth.
2. Pour in a glass and serve as your desire.

Nimboo Soda

Shikanjvi with a refreshing twist.

Serves 4

juice of 4 lemons (12 tbsp lemon juice)
2 teaspoons black salt
10 tbsp powdered sugar
1 tsp roasted cumin (*bhuna jeera*) powder
½ tsp black pepper powder
4 cups club soda (1 ltr. bottle)
ice cubes
4 sprigs of fresh mint leaves

1. Mix lemon juice, black salt, powdered sugar, roasted cumin powder and pepper.
2. Pour equal quantities of the mixture into four tall glasses.
3. Add mint leaves and ice cubes. Top each with a cup of club soda.

Strawberry Mint Smoothie

Serves 2

1 cup chopped strawberries
2 tbsp chopped mint leaves
2-3 tbsp powdered sugar, or to taste
4 tbsp vanilla ice cream
1 cup cold milk
1 cup any lemon drink

1. Blend strawberries, mint leaves and powdered sugar in a blender till smooth.
2. Add ice cream and milk to the blender and blend again. Pour into 2 glasses.
3. Top with any lemon drink. Serve garnished with mint and a strawberry.

Sherbet Angoori

Serves 4

4 cups black grape juice, ready made
3 tsp black salt
1½ tbsp tamarind pulp
10-12 crushed ice cubes

DRY ROAST TOGETHER
¾ tsp cumin seeds (*jeera*)
½ tsp carom seeds (*ajwain*)
1 tsp fennel seeds (*saunf*)

1. Dry-roast cumin seeds, carom seeds and fennel seeds. Grind all these with black salt to a fine powder.
2. Pour the grape juice into a jug. Add the ground spices and tamarind pulp and mix well.
3. Add the crushed ice and mix well.
4. Pour into glasses and serve.

Roasted Almond Milk Shake

Serves 4

20 almonds
2 cups chilled milk
3 tbsp powdered sugar, or to taste
a few ice cubes - crushed
a drop of red colour

GARNISH

a few pistachios and toasted almonds

1. Chop the almonds and roast in a pan for 3-4 minutes or till golden. Cool and grind to a powder.
2. Place the almond powder, sugar, colour, milk and the crushed ice in a blender and mix well.
3. Pour in a glass and garnish with a few pistachios and toasted almonds and serve.

Cool Flavour

Serves 2

2 cups cold milk
2 tbsp kesar-pista ice cream
½ cup vanilla ice cream
4 tbsp badam bahar syrup or thandai syrup
1 tsp powdered sugar
few ice cubes
2 tbsp falooda

GARNISH

1 tbsp almonds - cut into thin pieces
1 tbsp pistachio - cut into thin pieces
1 tbsp cashewnuts - cut into thin pieces
1 tbsp pomegranate seeds

1. Pour milk, kesar-pista ice cream, vanilla ice cream, badam bahar syrup, sugar and ice cubes in a mixer and blend 2-3 times.
2. Put falooda in a tall glass. Pour the blended milk.
3. Garnish with cashewnuts, pistachio, pomegranate seeds and serve.

Black Grape Cooler

Serves 6-8

½ kg black grapes
6 cups water
8 tbsp rose syrup, or to taste
1 tsp rock salt (*kala namak*)
few fresh mint leaves (*poodina*)

1. Place the washed grapes in a pressure cooker, add 6 cups water and pressure-cook to give 2 whistles. Remove from heat. When pressure drops open the lid, and let it cool to room temperature.
2. Place the mixture in a blender and blend till smooth. Strain the mixture.
3. Add rose syrup, salt and roughly chopped mint leaves to the grape juice. Chill.
4. To serve, place a few ice cubes in a glass, pour the cooler. Decorate with mint and grapes.

Summer Cool

An ideal drink for a hot summer lunch party. A two layered drink!

Serves 4

2½ cups (500 ml) guava juice, ready made
8 tbsp ginger ale
1½ cups chilled soda for topping
crushed ice

1. Take 4 tall stem glasses. Put lots of crushed ice in the glasses. Pour 2 tbsp ginger ale at the bottom of each glass.
2. Tilt the glass and gently pour guava juice, rolling along the sides of the glass.
3. Top each glass with 1/3 cup soda. Serve with a stirrer or a straw.

Kahwa

A saffron-scented special tea from Kashmir enriched with almonds.

Serves 4

2 tsp kahwa tea leaves or green tea leaves, crushed
5 green cardamoms (*chhoti illaichi*)
4" cinnamon (*dalchini*)
8 tsp sugar
2-3 saffron threads (*kesar*)
4-5 almonds, finely crushed

1. Pound cardamoms and cinnamon to a powder.
2. Pour 6 cups of water into a pan; add crushed kahwa tea leaves, cardamom-cinnamon powder, sugar and saffron. Bring to a boil.
3. Simmer for 3-4 minutes, or till the tea turns a pale gold.
4. Strain into teacups.
5. Sprinkle the almonds on top and serve hot.

Magaz Rose Lassi

Serves 2

1 cup (200 gm) yogurt
6 tbsp rose syrup, or to taste
2 tsp roasted melon seeds (*magaz*)
2 tbsp mint leaves - shredded
8-10 ice cubes
½ cup milk

GARNISH

2 tsp melon seeds (*magaz*) - roasted
2 tsp mint leaves - shredded
some rose syrup

1. Beat the yogurt with a fork till smooth.
2. Put the yogurt, rose syrup, mint leaves, milk and ice cubes in the mixer and blend till frothy.
3. Remove the jar and stir in the roasted magaz gently so as not to disturb the froth too much.
4. Pour the mixture into the lined glass and garnish with shredded mint leaves and roasted magaz. Drizzle some rose syrup on top.

Mango-Ginger Iced Tea

Serves 2

1" piece ginger - wash & thinly slice along with peel and crush lightly
¼ cup sugar
1¼ cups water
2 tea bags
8-10 mint leaves
1 cup mango juice
2 tsp lemon juice
1 cup crushed ice

GARNISH
mango slices, optional

1. Boil ginger slices, sugar and water. Simmer for 5 minutes. Dip the tea bags. Remove from fire. Leave for 2 minutes for the tea to brew well.
2. Strain and keep black ginger tea aside. Add mint leaves to ginger tea.
3. Cool the tea. Add mango juice and lemon juice. Mix well.
4. Put some ice in a glass. Pour the drink on ice and serve garnished with a mango slice.

Falooda

Enjoy it as a drink or a dessert.

Serves 6

1 small packet falooda
2 tbsp basil (*subzah*) seeds or *tookmalanga* (black oval seeds which when soaked develop a greyish, translucent, slippery coat)
4 cups milk
2 tbsp sugar
½ cup rose syrup, or to taste
6 scoops vanilla ice cream

1. Soak the subzah seeds in 1 cup milk. Chill the seeds in milk for about 30 minutes or even more till they swell.
2. Soak falooda in hot water for about 5 minutes until soft. Drain. Mix with 4 tbsp rose syrup. Keep covered in the refrigerator till serving time.
3. Add 2 tbsp sugar to the remaining 3 cups milk. Keep in the fridge to chill.
4. To serve, mix the milk with subzah seeds and whip well to mix the seeds. Divide it into 6 glasses.

5. Add some falooda in all the glasses.
6. Then gently pour in 2 tbsp rose syrup in each glass which being heavier will settle to the bottom.
7. Float a scoop of ice cream on top of each glass. Mix gently. Serve.

Zafran Sherbet

Serves 4-5

1 kg milk
10-12 saffron threads - soaked in
2 tbsp warm milk
3 tbsp sugar
¼ tsp green cardamom powder
10-12 almonds - blanched and cut into thin long slices
6-8 pistachios - blanched and cut into thin long slices
a few pinches of cinnamon powder
fresh rose petals to garnish

1. Boil milk and saffron in a thick-bottomed kadhai. Lower heat and simmer for 10 minutes.
2. Add sugar and cardamom powder and simmer for another 5-6 minutes.
3. Remove from heat, add almonds and pistachios and stir well. Set aside to cool. When completely cold, place in the refrigerator to chill.
4. Put ice in 4 glasses and divide sherbet among the glasses.
5. Top with a pinch of cinnamon. Swirl just once with a spoon. Serve garnished with a rose petal.

Papaya Honey Smoothie

Serves 2-3

1 cup chopped ripe papaya

1 cup cold milk

¾ cup thick yogurt

½ cup strawberry ice cream

4 tsp honey, or to taste

1. Put papaya and milk in a blender and blend till smooth. Add 8-10 ice cubes and blend again.
2. Add all the remaining ingredients and blend until thick and frothy. Serve cold.

Lemonade Delight

Serves 2

½ lemon - wash & cut into 4 pieces
¼ cup ginger ale
4 tbsp powdered sugar, or to taste
a pinch of black salt
½ cup chilled water
6-7 cubes of ice
¼ cup chilled soda

GARNISH

2 tbsp mint leaves - very finely chopped
a pinch of black pepper

1. Blend lemon pieces with ginger ale, powdered sugar, black salt, ½ cup cold water in a blender. Strain.
2. Put lemon-ginger ale in a glass.
3. Put ice in the glass.
4. Add some mint.
5. Top with soda & a pinch of black pepper.

Gajar ki Kanji

Celebrate Holi or any special occasion with this attractive drink – cold, sharp and spicy!

Serves 8

500 gm black carrots (*kali gajar*)
3 tsp salt
1 tsp black salt (*kala namak*)
¼ tsp asafoetida (*hing*)
2 tsp coarsely ground dry red chillies
3 tbsp ground mustard seeds (*rai*)
8-10 cups water

1. Peel, wash and cut the carrots into thin long fingers.
2. Mix carrots with all the other ingredients in a bowl.
3. Put in a glass jar, seal well and leave for 4-5 days to ferment at room temperature.
4. Put in the refrigerator till serving time. Serve chilled.

Note: If black carrots are not available then substitute them with regular carrots and a small beetroot.

The maturing of any kanji will depend upon the temperature; if the weather is warm the kanji will be ready earlier. Therefore keep checking every day.

Pink Lady

A little cream added to this drink gives it the special touch.

Serves 4-5

4 cups fresh watermelon juice
6 tbsp powdered sugar, or to taste
4 tsp cream/ice cream
4-5 fresh strawberries - chopped or
4 tsp lemon juice (both lend their sourness)

1. Cut the watermelon into small pieces. Put the pieces in a blender & blend for few seconds. Strain the juice to remove seeds.
2. Add sugar, fresh chopped strawberries (or lemon juice) and cream.
3. Blend again for a few seconds.
4. Fill 1/3 of the glass with crushed or cubed ice. Pour the prepared drink and garnish with a slit strawberry and a sprig of mint. Serve.

Purple Rain

It's just heavenly! You can almost feel the cool rain pouring down.

Serves 4

½ kg black grapes
2 tsp lemon juice
4 tbsp powdered sugar, or to taste
4 tsp cream or vanilla ice cream
a bottle of soda - chilled
ice cubes or crushed ice
for garnishing - grape and mint sprigs

1. Place the grapes with ¾ cup of water and blend in a blender. Strain to get 2 large cups of juice. Keep aside in the refrigerator.
2. Mix grape juice, lemon juice, sugar and ice cream in a pan and refrigerate.
3. At serving time, blend for a few seconds. Add about 1 cup soda to the blended mixture. Mix with a spoon. Pour into a glass over ice.

Khus Punch

Serves 1

1 cup chilled water
1 tsp lemon juice
2 pinches of black salt
3 tbsp powdered sugar, or to taste
2-3 tsp khus syrup

GARNISH
2 tsp grated apple

1. Put all the ingredients in a mixer and blend till smooth.
2. Pour in a glass and top with grated apple. Serve.

Adraki Shikanjvi

Serves 4

6 tbsp lemon juice
2 tbsp ginger juice
2 tsp roasted cumin powder
½ tsp salt, or to taste
½ tsp black salt, or to taste
½ cup sugar, ice cubes
4 cups chilled water

TO GARNISH
1 medium lemon, sliced

1. Boil ½ cup sugar and ½ cup water. Simmer for 2 minutes and remove from fire. Cool.
2. Mix together ginger juice, lemon juice, roasted cumin powder, salt, black salt and sugar syrup in a large jug.
3. Add 4 cups of chilled water and stir. Pour into glasses with lemon slices.

Indian Desserts

Malpuas

The batter should be prepared at least one hour before frying the malpuas.

Makes 8-10

8 tbsp plain flour (*maida*)
4 tbsp semolina (*suji*)
1/3 cup sugar, ½ cup water
1 cup milk, approx.
½ tsp fennel (*saunf*) - crushed
¼ tsp green cardamom (*elaichi*) powder
2 big pinches baking powder
oil/ghee for shallow frying

SOAKING SYRUP

1¼ cups sugar, 1 cup water
a few strands of saffron (*kesar*)

1. Make a sugar syrup by boiling 1/3 cup sugar and ½ cup water. Simmer on low heat for 2 minutes till sugar dissolves. Remove from fire. Keep aside.
2. Mix maida and suji. Add hot sugar syrup and mix well. Add milk gradually, adding enough to get a smooth batter which is of a thick pouring consistency and which coats the back of a spoon. Add elaichi and saunf. Add baking powder and mix.
3. For soaking syrup, boil sugar, water and kesar. Simmer for 4-5 minutes to make a syrup of sticky consistency. Remove from heat and keep aside to cool down to room temperature.
4. In a frying pan heat oil/ghee about ½" height. If the oil/ghee is too much, puas will start floating. Let the oil be medium hot.
5. Pour about half of a big laddle of batter in the ghee. Let it spread on its own. Fry on medium heat till golden brown at the edges. Then turn with a chimta (tongs) and reduce heat. Fry till golden brown on both sides and the edges acquire a rich brown colour.
6. Remove from oil/ghee and put it in the soaking syrup for 1-2 minutes, turning side to coat both sides. Remove from syrup and serve with rabri if you like.

Payasam

Fine vermicelli cooked in ghee, sugar and milk and garnished with fried nuts and raisins.

Serves 6

4 cups full cream milk
½ cup water
¼ cup rose syrup, or to taste
1 cup broken vermicelli (*seviyaan*)
2 tbsp *ghee*
1 tbsp broken cashewnut pieces (*kaju tukda*)
2 tbsp raisins
seeds of 3-4 green cardamoms (*illaichi*) - powdered

1. Heat ghee. Fry cashewnut pieces & raisins, remove from ghee & keep aside.
2. Add seviyaan to the remaining ghee in the pan. Fry to a light brown colour, add water, cook for just a minute, on low heat.
3. Now add the milk gradually, stirring.
4. Continue to cook until payasam is quite thick for about 10-12 minutes on low flame. Remove from fire.
5. Add rose syrup. Check sweetness and add as per your taste.
6. Add cardamom, nuts & raisins. Mix well. Serve hot or cold.

Anjeer Ice Cream

Serves 8

10 dry figs (*anjeer*) - finely chopped and soaked in 4 tbsp milk for 1-2 hours
3 tbsp honey
1 kg full cream milk
2 tbsp cornflour - dissolve in ¼ cup milk
¾ cup rose syrup, or to taste
1 cup (200 gm) cream

1. Boil milk in a heavy bottom kadhai. Keep on medium flame for 30 minutes till slightly thick.
2. Add cornflour paste & cook for 5 minutes, stirring continuously. Remove from fire. Let it cool.
3. Add rose syrup. Set this thickened rose syrup-milk overnight or for 6-8 hours.
4. Next day, cut the set rose syrup-milk into small cubes. Beat till fluffy. Do not let it melt while beating.
5. Beat cream till fluffy. Add the whipped cream to it and mix for just a few seconds. Do not let the mixture melt.

6. Add soaked figs and honey. Mix. Transfer to an aluminium container. Cover tightly with a lid or aluminium foil. Freeze overnight to set well.

Coconut Suji Ladoo

Makes 40 pieces

3 cups semolina (*suji*)
¾ cup *ghee*
1 cup milk
2 cups sugar
2 cups desiccated coconut
6 cardamom (*illaichi*) seeds - crushed
or 1 tsp cardamom powder

TO COAT

½ cup desiccated coconut
¼ tsp kesar - soaked in 1 tbsp hot water
1 tsp green pista - shredded

1. Dry roast semolina in a *kadhai* on medium heat for 2 minutes.
2. Add *ghee* and cook for about 4 minutes till semolina is slightly brown and gives a cooked flavour.
3. Add the milk and mix well. Remove from heat. Keep aside.
4. In a separate pan put 1 *cup* water and sugar. Cook on medium heat to 1 string syrup (do not bring to 2 string as the ladoo will harden). This takes about 3-4 minutes after the boil.
5. Pour this syrup on the semolina mixture and mix.

6. Add coconut and cardamom and mix again. Cool slightly.
7. When still warm make ladoos. Roll in desiccated coconut to coat. Dot with soaked kesar and sprinkle pista. Serve.

Rasgulla Pudding

Serves 6

10-15 small rasgullas, preferably tinned rasgullas
¼ cup seeds of pomegranate (*anar ke dane*)
500 gm kesar pista ice cream
1 tbsp finely chopped pista
1 tbsp finely chopped almonds
½ cup cold milk
1 tsp saffron (*kesar*) - soaked in 1 tbsp rose water

1. Squeeze rasgulls to remove all sugar syrup. (Handle them with care or they will break). Make a small hole in the centre by scooping a little.

2. Fill 7-8 seeds of pomegranate and arrange in a flat serving dish.

3. Put ice-cream, milk, kesar and pulp of rasgullas in the grinder and grind 3-4 times. Pour on the rasgullas in the serving dish.

4. Garnish with pista and almonds and cool in the fridge before serving.

Fruit & Ice

Serves 4

2 bananas - cubed, 2 mangoes - cubed
1 cup deseeded and cubed watermelon (*tarbooz*)
1 cup cubed fresh pineapple
juice of 1 lemon, lots of crushed ice
½ cup coconut cream or ¼ cup cream + ¼ cup coconut milk
2 tbsp sugar, 2 tbsp water

1. Put the fruits in a bowl.
2. Pour the lemon juice over the fruits to prevent them from getting discoloured.
3. Add crushed ice.
4. Pile fruit-ice mixture into 4 individual ice-cream glasses or bowls. Place the fruit-ice glasses in the freezer. Keep chilled.
5. Combine sugar and water in a pan. Bring to a boil. Simmer for about 3-4 minutes so that the sugar gets dissolved and the mixture and becomes syrupy.
6. Add the sugar syrup (to taste) to the coconut cream mixture.
7. Whisk the cream-syrup mixture.
8. Just before serving, drizzle cream-syrup mixture over the fruit-ice. Serve immediately.

Duet Ice Cream

Makes 4

2 cups ready made mango juice
8 tbsp sugar
2 cups (400 gm) cream
½-1 cup rose syrup, or to taste

1. Beat cream till thick. Add ½ cup rose syrup and mix. Check sweetness. Add more rose syrup if needed.
2. Transfer cream to kulfi moulds filling them only half. Cover with lid and keep upright in the freezer for 2 hours to semi set.
3. After the pink ice cream is semi set, insert the ice cream stick. Freeze upright till firm.
4. Boil 8 tbsp sugar with ½ cup water. Simmer for 2 minutes. Add mango juice to the above sugar syrup. Mix. Cool the mix in the freezer for 10 minutes.
5. Pour the cooled mango mixture on top of set pink ice cream. Cover with aluminium foil and freeze overnight.

Biscuit Pudding

Serves 4

16 Marie biscuits
aluminium foil

MIXTURE

4 tbsp milk
1 tbsp powdered sugar
2 tbsp drinking chocolate powder
1 tbsp coffee powder
1 tbsp cocoa powder

PASTE

2 tbsp flour (*maida*), 8 tbsp icing sugar
2 tbsp drinking chocolate powder
6 tbsp white butter - softened

1. Put all the ingredients of the mixture in a bowl and mix well to get pouring consistency.
2. Put all the ingredients of the paste in a bowl, mix well to get a thick paste.
3. Dip marie biscuit in the mixture and overlap one by one, 8 biscuits like a sandwich.
4. Apply paste on all sides of the biscuit well with the help of spoon. Wrap in aluminium foil from all sides. Use the remaining ingredients also the same way.
5. Keep in a refrigerator for 3-4 hours to freeze. When the biscuits are frozen properly then remove from foil and cut into four to get triangular pieces. Decorate with glace cherries and almonds. Serve.

Anjeer aur Nariyal ki Barfi

Makes 15

¼ kg *dry figs (anjeer)* - wash & chop finely
1 liter milk
½ cup grated dry coconut
½ tsp cardamom (*illaichi*) powder (seeds of 4-5 green cardamoms - crushed)
4 tbsp sugar
1 tsp *ghee*
pista slices to garnish

1. Heat milk in heavy bottom *kadhai* add the chopped *anjeer* and cook on medium heat till the milk turns thick. Sometimes the milk looks curdled but just keep stirring constantly till thick.

2. Mash the *anjeer* with the back of the *kadchi* while cooking to get a slightly pulpy and almost dry paste. This takes about 25 minutes on medium flame.

3. Add the sugar, coconut, cardamom powder and *ghee*, cook till the mixture leaves the side of the *kadhai* and collects. Set in a small 8" tray. Garnish with pista slices and cut into squares.

Rose Shahi Tukri

Makes 16

4 bread slices - remove sides

TOPPING

100 gm *paneer* - finely grated
4 tsp rose syrup, or to taste
¼ tsp green cardamom powder
(*chhoti illaichi*)
4 tbsp finely chopped mixed nuts

TO SERVE

rabdi (page 77, but without sugar)
mixed with some rose syrup

1. For the topping, mix paneer, illaichi powder, nuts with 4 tsp rose syrup in a bowl.
2. Cut each slice into 4 triangles. Deep fry bread slices till golden and crisp.
3. Spread some rose syrup over each fried bread slice.
4. Place ½ tbsp topping mixture over each bread slice. Spread some unsweetened rabdi mixed with rose syrup in a flat serving platter. Place tukri over it to serve.

Jalebi with Rabri

What can be more tempting than homemade hot jalebis served with thick rabri?

Makes 1 kg.

JALEBI
250 gm plain flour (*maida*)
25 gm gram flour (*besan*)
1 tbsp oil, 1 cup curd
1½ cups water

SUGAR SYRUP
350 gm sugar, 2 cups water
2-3 pinches yellow colour
4-6 threads saffron (*kesar*)
500 gm ghee for deep frying

1. Mix together the flours, oil and curds. Add water to make a medium thick paste of soft dropping consistency. Beat well with an electric hand mixer. Cover and keep aside for 6-8 hours in summers or overnight in winters for fermentation. If fermented extra, the batter may turn sour and the jalebis will not be so good.

2. Prepare a two string syrup with the sugar and water. Feel the syrup between the finger and thumb to check the strings. When a 2 string syrup is dropped from a spoon, it falls in two separate drops. Add colour and saffron.

3. Heat ghee in a big non stick frying pan. Beat the mixture well with a spoon. Fill in a thick plastic bag. Cut a small hole in a corner. Alternately use an icing bag with a writing nozzle. Squeeze batter and drop medium sized whirls in a continuous flow beginning from outer circle and ending in the centre. This will give better shape to the jalebies. Keep slight space between the circles, do not overlap.

4. Fry them for 2-3 minutes till golden brown on both sides. Drain and drop in the hot syrup for 2-3 minutes. Serve.

RABRI

4 cups full cream milk, 2 tbsp sugar
75 gm *khoya* - grated (½ cup)
3 green cardamoms (*chhoti illaichi*) - powdered
6-8 pistas - chopped

Boil milk in a heavy bottomed kadhai. Add khoya and sugar. Simmer on low-medium heat for about 40-45 minutes, scraping the sides, till the quantity is reduced to almost half and the mixture turns thick with a thick pouring consistency. Remove from fire.

The rabri turns thick on keeping. Add some chopped pistas and cardamom powdered into the mixture. Serve hot or cold by itself or with jalebis.

Baadshahi Kulfi

Serves 15

1 kg (5 cups) full cream milk - at room temperature

1 tin (400 gms) milkmaid (condensed milk)

15 almonds, 15 pistachios

2 tbsp cornflour

¼ tsp kesar (*saffron*) - soak in 1 tbsp warm milk

3-4 green cardamoms (*chhoti illaichi*) - crushed

1 tbsp pistachio and almonds - shredded

1 tbsp raisins (*kishmish*)

TO DRIZZLE

2-3 tbsp rose syrup, or to taste

1. Blanch almonds and pistachios by boiling in water for 2-3 minutes. Remove skin. Grind to a paste with 2-3 tbsp milk.
2. Dissolve cornflour in ¼ cup milk.
3. Transfer milkmaid in a heavy-bottom kadhai. Add the remaining milk gradually to the milkmaid, stirring continuously. Mix well. Add green cardamom & kesar. Keep on fire. Boil, stirring continuously.
4. Add the cornflour paste to the boiling milk, stirring continuously. Simmer on low heat for about 10 minutes. Remove from fire. Add almond paste. Cool.
5. Add shredded pistachios, almonds and raisins. Fill in clean kulfi moulds and leave to set in the freezer for 6-8 hours or overnight. Serve drizzled with rose syrup.

Makhane ki Rose Kheer

A dessert of lotus seeds.

Serves 8-10

2 kg milk
100 gm lotus seeds (*makhane*) - roast for 2-3 minutes in a pan
½ cup rose syrup, or to taste
½ tsp green cardamom (*chhoti illaichi)* powder
1 tbsp chopped green pista

1. Roast the lotus seeds till they start to change colour. Let them cool. Crush half of them, leaving the other half whole.
2. Boil milk. When the milk starts to boil, add the lotus seeds and cook in milk at medium heat, stirring every now & then. Cook till the lotus seeds are cooked and the consistency of the milk reduced by one third. Remove from heat.
3. Add rose syrup to taste and sprinkle crushed cardamom. Mix well. Transfer to a serving dish. Decorate with silver leaves and chopped pista.

Paneer aur Petha ka Peda

Makes 45-50 small pedas

125 gm *khoya* - grate finely (1½ cups)
250 gm *paneer* - grate finely (3 cups)
300 gm *mitha agra ka petha/ dry petha* - grate finely (1½ cups)
250 gm (2½ cups) desiccated coconut (*bura nariyal*)
1 tsp rose water or a few drops of rose essence
yellow colour
pista to garnish

1. Grate the *paneer* and mitha *agra ka petha* (shown on extreme left in the picture). Keep aside.

2. Heat a thick bottom non-stick *kadhai* or pan. Add the *khoya* and cook for 1-2 minutes till soft but does not change colour, remove from heat and cool slightly.

3. Add the grated *paneer* and *petha* to the *khoya*. Add 200 gm of desiccated coconut (reserve 50 gm for coating) to the khoya. Mix very well till smooth.

Contd...

4. Add colour and flavouring and mix well again.
5. Shape small peda's. Roll in the reserved nariyal. Make a light depression with the ring finger. Garnish with pista in the depression. Refrigerate till serving time. Serve at room temperature.

Moong Dal Halwa

Makes 1.5 kg

500 gm (2½ cups) whole, split green beans (*hari moong tukra dal*)
650 gm (3 cups) *ghee*
450 gm (2¼ cups) sugar
1 litre (5 cups) milk
½ tsp green cardamoms (*chhoti illaichi*) powder
8-10 threads saffron (*kesar*) soaked in 2 tbsp hot water
50 gm (4 tbsp) cashew nuts
25 gm (2 tbsp) almonds
2 tbsp raisins (*kishmish*)

FOR DECORATION
1 silver sheet (*varak*)

1. Soak *dal* overnight. Wash, rub and remove the green skin. Drain and grind it, using as little water as possible.
2. Heat 500 gm of *ghee* in a *kadahi*. Add the ground paste in *ghee* and fry on a medium to slow flame for 45-50 minutes, stirring continuously.
3. When it turns pink in colour, dries and the *ghee* separates, add sugar and milk.
4. Cook the mixture on a slow flame. Keep stirring for 10 minutes.
5. When the mixture dries up again, add the remaining ghee. Fry for 5-7 minutes. Add half the chopped dry fruits and saffron water.
6. Remove from the fire. Decorate with remaining dry fruits, cardamom and the silver sheet.

Kalakand

Makes 10 pieces

1 litre rich buffalo milk
80 gm sugar, (slightly less than ½ cup)
2 pinches tartaric powder
1 teaspoon cornflour
6-8 threads saffron dissolved in 1 tbsp of hot water

DECORATION

seeds of 4 green cardamoms (*illaichi*)
- powdered
4 pistas - chopped

1. Boil milk in a kadhai. Add sugar. Mix well. Add tartaric powder pinch by pinch till the milk curdles slightly. Very tiny granules should stick at the back of the spoon. The milk does not curdle fully and there is no green whey (water) seen.

2. Keep boiling on high flame, stirring constantly. Boil for about 12 minutes till the mixture thickens. Reduce the flame. When the mixture becomes semi-solid and frothy sprinkle cornflour over it. Mix well. Do not dry the mixture. Total cooking time for this step is about 15 minutes.

3. Turn the mixture onto a greased tray. Spread a 1½" thick even layer in the small baking tray or a plastic tiffin box.
4. Decorate with cardamoms and pista. Let it set for 2-3 hours. Do not refrigerate.
5. Cut into squares. Store in the refrigerator.

TIP: If you add too much tartaric powder, the milk curdles fully and the greenish water separates. This makes the *chenna* hard and chewy. The mixture should be milky (whitish) in colour and semi-dry when removed from fire. If you dry the mixture too much and then set, it becomes like milk cake.

Besan ki Burfi

Makes 24 pieces

250 gm (2¾ cups) gramflour (*besan*)
150 gm (1 cup) powdered sugar
150 gm (¾ cup) pure ghee
3-4 green cardamoms (*chhoti illaichi*)
- powder

Note: To make besan ladoo, increase the *besan* to 3 cups.

1. In a heavy bottomed pan, put gramflour. Dry roast gramflour for about 10 minutes on low heat, stirring continuously till it gives a roasted smell.

2. Add ghee. Cook on very low heat for about 15 minutes till golden. Do not make it brown. Make it just golden with a hint of brown. Remove from fire. Add sugar and mix well.

3. Transfer to a greased *thali*. Press well to smoothen. Sprinkle cardamom powder. Leave to set for 5-6 hours at room temperature in a cool place but not in the refrigerator. You can leave it over night to set well. Cut into 1" pieces.

Hyderabadi Cookies

> **Makes 20**

1½ cups plain flour (*maida*)
4 tbsp rose syrup, or to taste
¼ tsp soda bi carb (*mitha soda*)
1/3 cup white butter
1½ tbsp candied fruit (*Tuti Fruiti*)

1. Mix flour with soda.
2. Beat butter well.
3. Add flour, rose syrup and *Tutu Fruiti* to the butter. Mix well to form a soft dough.
4. Roll dough between 2 sheets of plastic paper to ¼" thickness. Cut into squares.
5. Bake cookies in a moderate oven at 160° C for 25 minutes. Cool on a wire rack. Store in an air tight container.

Atta Pinnie

Makes 15-20

250 gm (2¼ cups) wheat flour (*atta*)
300 gm (1¾ cups melted) *desi ghee*
250 gm (2 cups) powdered sugar, preferably *bhura chini*
4-5 tbsp milk (cold)
seeds of 10 green cardamoms - crushed into powder
a few sliced pistas to garnish

1. Melt ghee in a heavy bottom pan.
2. Add atta & cook for 12-15 minutes on low flame, stir continuously, till medium brown in colour. When aroma exudes and the flour is properly browned, take off the fire.
3. Immediately spread in a tray. Cool till it comes to room temperature. Sprinkle cardamom and add sugar. Mix well.
4. Sprinkle milk and mix well again to get a mixture that binds well.
5. Form tight fist (*mutthi*) shaped pinnies. This is done by taking some mixture and pressing it in the fist. Garnish with pista.

Kesari Sandesh

Makes 12

CHHENA

1 litre full cream milk
2 tbsp white vinegar

OTHER INGREDIENTS

3 tbsp sugar
1 tsp flour (*maida*)
¼ tsp saffron (*kesar*) - dissolved in 2 tbsp hot water,
few sliced green pista
a few cloves (*laung*), optional

1. Boil milk. Remove from fire. Add enough vinegar to curdle the milk. As soon as the milk curdles, add 1 bottle (5-6 cups) water to the chhena to bring down the temperature. This prevents overcooking of the chhena and helps it to remain soft.

2. Immediately strain through a muslin cloth. Squeeze completely to remove excess water.

3. Add the sugar and maida to the chhena. Add the kesar water, keeping the strands for topping. Mix gently.

4. Cook this mixture on a very low flame in a heavy kadhai stirring continuously for 5-6 minutes. Keep spreading the chhena on the sides of the kadhai, as the centre bottom of the kadhai gets the maximum heat. It is cooked on very low heat and with continuous stirring.

If the chhena gets over heated, fat will separate and it will get grainy. Remove the kadhai from the flame at regular intervals so as not to overheat the chhena. The sandesh mixture is ready when neither too dry nor too moist.

5. Remove from fire to a plate to cool. Mash with palm. If needed, add 1-2 tsp milk gradually.

6. Shape into flat discs of ½" thickness. Press a finger on kesar strand and put on each sandesh. You can also put into moulds, like the pineapple mould, stick a clove for the stem and pista as the leaves as shown. You can also add colour to the mixture and make triangles as shown. Draw lines by dipping a tooth pick in colour and make impression on the sweet.

Mewa ke Ladoo

Makes 20-25

2 cups plain flour (*maida*)
1 cup semolina (*suji*)
1 cup *ghee*
2 cups desiccated powdered nariyal
100 gm khoya - grated
1 cup sugar powdered
seeds of 10-12 green cardamoms (*chhoti illaichi*) - crushed to a powder
1 cup dry fruits - cashewnuts (*kaju*), raisins (*kishmish*), almond (*badam*) - chopped

1. Heat a *kadhai* and dry roast semolina for about 7-8 minutes on low-medium heat till light brown. Keep aside.
2. Heat *ghee* in a *kadhai*, add plain flour and cook on medium to low heat for about 5 minutes till light brown, and looses raw flavour. Add semolina and mix well for a minute. Remove from fire.
3. After the mixture cools down, add khoya and mix well. Add nariyal, cardamom powder, sugar and chopped nuts. Mix well. Add 1 more tbsp of melted ghee if needed to bind properly.
4. Now immediately bind into laddoos, they will firm up when cool.

Suji ka Halwa

Serves 4

1 cup semolina (*suji*)
½ cup *desi ghee*
1 cup sugar, 1 cup milk
3 cups water
4 green cardamom (*chhoti illaichi*) - skinned and crushed
a pinch of yellow colour
8-10 raisins (*kishmish*)
1 tbsp *pista* - cut into thin long pieces
8-10 almonds - cut into thin long pieces

1. Mix milk, water, *kishmish*, crushed *illaichi*, yellow colour and sugar. Boil. Remove from fire. Stir to dissolve the sugar. Keep aside.
2. Heat *ghee* in a *kadahi*. Fry *suji* on low heat till it just changes its colour.
3. Add milk mixture, stirring continuously for 7-8 minutes till the halwa leaves the sides of the *kadahi*. Remove from fire.
4. Keep in a serving dish. Decorate with shredded almonds and *pista*. Serve hot.

Herbs & Spices

ENGLISH NAME	HINDI NAME	ENGLISH NAME	HINDI NAME
1. Asafoetida	1. Hing	18. Fenugreek Seeds	18. Methi Dana
2. Bay Leaves	2. Tej Patta	19. Fenugreek Leaves, Dried	19. Kasuri Methi
3. Cardamom	3. Illaichi, Chhoti Illaichi	20. Garam Masala Powder	20. Garam Masala
4. Cardamom, Black	4. Moti Illaichi	21. Garlic	21. Lahsun
5. Carom Seeds	5. Ajwain	22. Ginger	22. Adrak
6. Chillies, Green	6. Hari Mirch	23. Mace	23. Javitri
7. Chillies, Dry Red	7. Sukhi Sabut Lal Mirch	24. Mango Powder, Dried	24. Amchur
8. Chilli Powder, Red	8. Lal Mirch Powder	25. Melon Seeds	25. Magaz
9. Cinnamon	9. Dalchini	26. Mint Leaves	26. Pudina
10. Cloves	10. Laung	27. Mustard Seeds	27. Rai, Sarson
11. Coriander Seeds	11. Sabut Dhania	28. Nigella, Onion Seeds	28. Kalaunji
12. Coriander Seeds, ground	12. Dhania Powder	29. Nutmeg	29. Jaiphal
13. Coriander Leaves	13. Hara Dhania	30. Peppercorns	30. Sabut Kali Mirch
14. Cumin Seeds	14. Jeera	31. Pomegranate Seeds, Dried	31. Anardana
15. Cumin Seeds, black	15. Shah Jeera	32. Sesame Seeds	32. Til
16. Curry Leaves	16. Kari Patta	33. Saffron	33. Kesar
17. Fennel Seeds	17. Saunf	34. Turmeric Powder	34. Haldi

INTERNATIONAL CONVERSION GUIDE

These are not exact equivalents; they've been rounded-off to make measuring easier.

WEIGHTS & MEASURES

METRIC	IMPERIAL
15 g	½ oz
30 g	1 oz
60 g	2 oz
90 g	3 oz
125 g	4 oz (¼ lb)
155 g	5 oz
185 g	6 oz
220 g	7 oz
250 g	8 oz (½ lb)
280 g	9 oz
315 g	10 oz
345 g	11 oz
375 g	12 oz (¾ lb)
410 g	13 oz
440 g	14 oz
470 g	15 oz
500 g	16 oz (1 lb)
750 g	24 oz (1½ lb)
1 kg	30 oz (2 lb)

LIQUID MEASURES

METRIC	IMPERIAL
30 ml	1 fluid oz
60 ml	2 fluid oz
100 ml	3 fluid oz
125 ml	4 fluid oz
150 ml	5 fluid oz (¼ pint/1 gill)
190 ml	6 fluid oz
250 ml	8 fluid oz
300 ml	10 fluid oz (½ pint)
500 ml	16 fluid oz
600 ml	20 fluid oz (1 pint)
1000 ml	1¾ pints

CUPS & SPOON MEASURES

METRIC	IMPERIAL
1 ml	¼ tsp
2 ml	½ tsp
5 ml	1 tsp
15 ml	1 tbsp
60 ml	¼ cup
125 ml	½ cup
250 ml	1 cup

HELPFUL MEASURES

METRIC	IMPERIAL
3 mm	1/8 in
6 mm	¼ in
1 cm	½ in
2 cm	¾ in
2.5 cm	1 in
5 cm	2 in
6 cm	2½ in
8 cm	3 in
10 cm	4 in
13 cm	5 in
15 cm	6 in
18 cm	7 in
20 cm	8 in
23 cm	9 in
25 cm	10 in
28 cm	11 in
30 cm	12 in (1ft)

HOW TO MEASURE

When using the graduated metric measuring cups, it is important to shake the dry ingredients loosely into the required cup. Do not tap the cup on the table, or pack the ingredients into the cup unless otherwise directed. Level top of cup with a knife. When using graduated metric measuring spoons, level top of spoon with a knife. When measuring liquids in the jug, place jug on a flat surface, check for accuracy at eye level.

OVEN TEMPERATURE

These oven temperatures are only a guide. Always check the manufacturer's manual.

	°C (Celsius)	°F (Fahrenheit)	Gas Mark
Very low	120	250	1
Low	150	300	2
Moderately low	160	325	3
Moderate	180	350	4
Moderately high	190	375	5
High	200	400	6
Very high	230	450	7